T0128637

Zola Discovers South Africa's

by Alexandria Pereira

AuthorHouse™
1663 Liberty Drive
Bloomington, IN 47403
www.authorhouse.com
Phone: 833-262-8899

Because of the dynamic nature of the Internet, any web addresses or links contained in this book may have changed since publication and may no longer be valid. The views expressed in this work are solely those of the author and do not necessarily reflect the views of the publisher, and the publisher hereby disclaims any responsibility for them.

This book is printed on acid-free paper.

ISBN: 978-1-6655-7325-2 (sc)
ISBN: 978-1-6655-7326-9 (hc)
ISBN: 978-1-6655-7324-5 (e)

Library of Congress Control Number: 2022919055

Print information available on the last page.

Published by AuthorHouse 10/19/2022

authorHOUSE®

The Mystery of History Series

South Africa

Book 4 of 4

Dedication

To my grandma, whose life work was dedicated
to children and their pursuit of knowledge.

"Would you like some lunch, Zola?" asked Grandma.

"Sure, Grandma," replied Zola.

"What are you painting today?" asked Grandma.

"The giraffe I saw when we were driving to the museum. I want to show my friends how the giraffe ate leaves from a really tall tree," replied Zola.

"Did you know, Zola, that our ancestors did the same thing? They would paint the animals they saw on cave walls. Then they would use those painted animals to tell stories to their friends," said Grandma.

"Really?" said Zola.

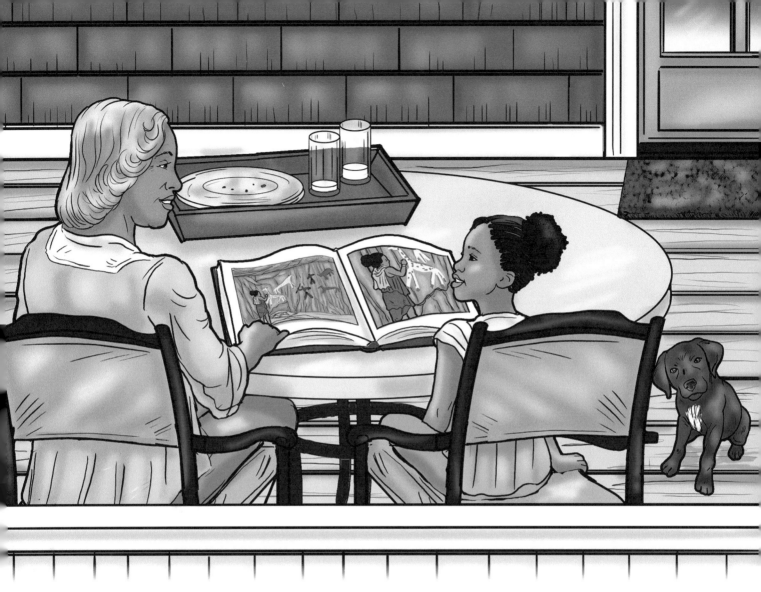

"Yes. After something exciting happened, people would tell stories about it to one another. Because there were no books to read, or even paper to paint on, people would paint on the walls of caves where they lived. They would use those paintings to tell stories. This was their way of teaching their children and grandchildren about the world.

People painted animals and people on cave walls and told stories to one another for almost 100,000 years," said Grandma.

"But Grandma, where did they get paint from?" asked Zola.

"Well, Zola, there were no stores or paints to buy 100,000 years ago. They didn't even have paintbrushes like we have today. People learned to make paints by grinding pieces of ochre and charcoal and mixing them with water. They used very thin animal bones as paintbrushes or used their hands and fingers.

They kept their art supplies in big seashells, like this.

"Our ancestors continued to paint. This is one of the most famous of our ancestor's paintings. It is called The Linton Panel. Our ancestors also learned to make things out of clay like statues and animal figures. They discovered how to melt gold and form it into many shapes. They invented dances and music to tell stories. They even carved and painted stones to share their ideas with one another. This helped people work better together.

"As more and more people were born, there were more and more people all trying to work together. It was hard for all these people to share, and they started arguing.

Then the Industrial Revolution started, people learned new things and had new ideas, and started working together again.

"With new ideas about science and engineering, South African people discovered diamonds and more gold. They built mines and factories to make all sorts of new things.

"With new ideas about engineering and technology, they built small towns and big cities.

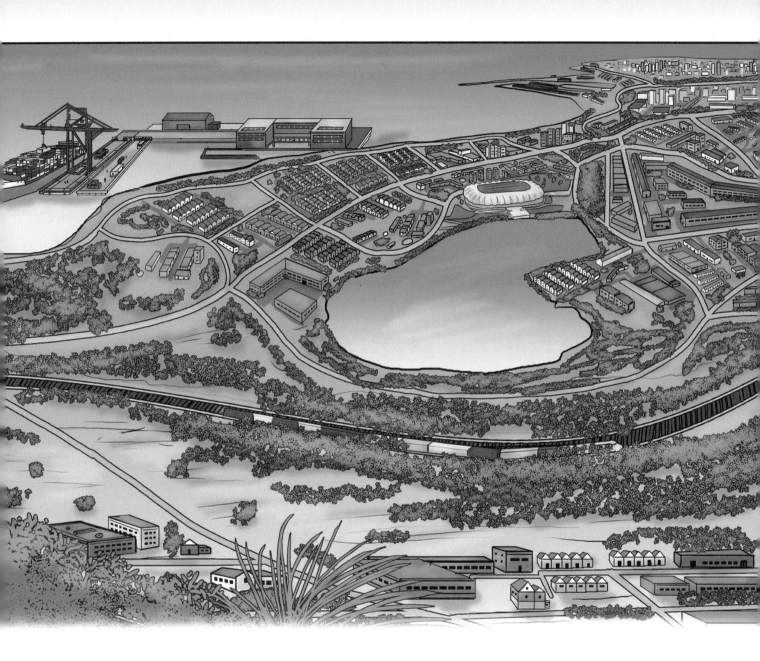

They also built roads, railroads, stadiums, and places for ships to dock and trade.

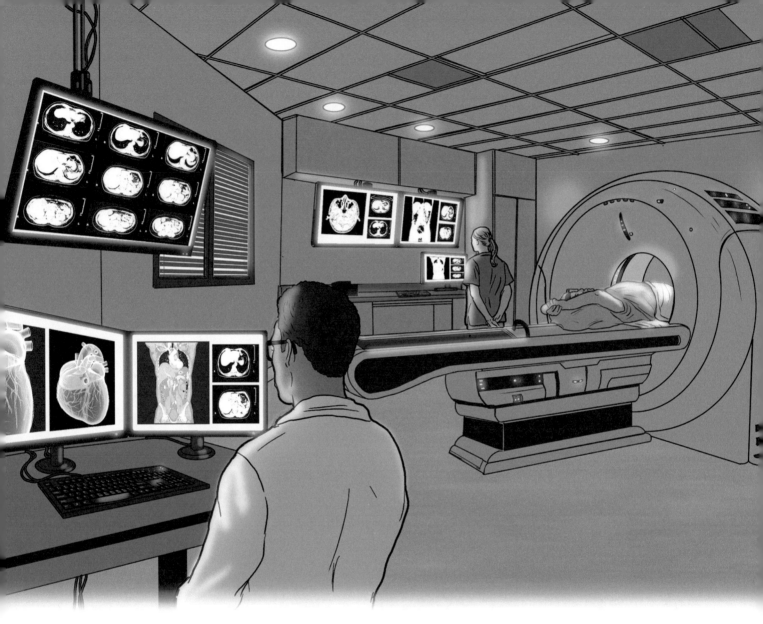

"With new ideas about science and medicine, one South African man, invented a way for doctors to replace a person's sick heart with a new, healthy heart. This is called a heart transplant.

Two South African men invented the CAT scan, which uses a special X-ray machine that takes three-dimensional images of the inside of someone's body so that a doctor can see how to help that person feel better.

"Another South African man invented a glue that was so special it was used to hold pieces of a spacecraft, the Apollo 11 Eagle landing craft, that first landed on the moon in 1969.

"And scientists from around the world are working with other scientists in South Africa to make and operate a network of radio telescopes. These telescopes can see and hear into space, farther and clearer than before. It is called the Square Kilometer Array (SKA) project.

"South Africa still has a lot of problems to solve, but now all the people get to choose the government and make the rules. The people of South Africa continue to grow, and have new ideas, as they learn to work together to solve problems and make life better for themselves," said Grandma.

"Wow, Grandma! The South African people, my ancestors, started out painting animals on cave walls. Because they worked hard, learned new things, and invented new ways to do things, I am here learning about the mystery that is my South African history.

"Thank you, Grandma," said Zola.

"You are welcome, Zola," said Grandma.

Educational Support Activities for Adults to Engage with Children

Basic Human Needs
We need food to grow.
We need clothing to keep us warm.
We need shelter to keep us safe and dry.
We need to socialize to work together.
We need to solve problems so we can invent and be creative.

Practical Life and Sensorial Foundation
Plant a seed. Grind some wheat to make flour. Why do these things?

History
Make up a song or a dance and tell a story about something that happened to you.

Science
Paint rocks using crushed charcoal and natural pigments. Use twigs or your hands and fingers for brushes.

Geography and Map Work
Find the Continent of Africa on a map. Find South Africa on the African Continent.
Trace South Africa and draw significant landforms, mountains, rivers, plateaus, beaches, etc.
Draws lines of migration into South Africa.

Language
Make up a new language using signs or clicks. What are you saying?

Peace Curriculum
What ideas do you have to work better together with your friends?

South African Timeline

3 million BC	The first human ancestors, the *Australopithecus afarensis*, appear in the Cradle of Humankind, situated in today's South Africa.
300,000 BC - 300	AD First *Homo sapiens* inhabited parts of South Africa.
1488 AD	Portuguese explorer Bartolomeu Dias sails around the southern tip of Africa, the Cape of Good Hope, and Khoekhoe establish trade with Europeans.
1497	Vasco da Gama arrives at the Cape of Good Hope on his way to India.
1500's	Portuguese ships land at Table Bay. The Bantu farmers and herdsmen establish trade with the Europeans.
1652	The Dutch East India Company establishes the Dutch Cape Colony.
1663	More European sailors establish a settlement at Saldanha Bay.
1795	The British take control of Cape Colony.
1802	The Dutch regain control of Cape Colony.
1806	The British regain control of Cape Colony.
1814	The Dutch formally give the Cape to Britain.
1833	The Great Trek begins, as 6,000 Dutch settlers, called Boers, migrated eastward from the Cape Colony.
1867	Diamonds are discovered in the Orange Free State at Kimberley.
1885	The Cape-to-Kimberley railroad was completed.
1886	Gold is discovered and the Witwatersrand Gold Rush starts.

1893 - 1914	Mahatma Gandhi started his nonviolent, noncompliance methods helping India's working in the Transvaal protest against the government's Pass Laws, Black Act.
1934	The Status of the Union Act declares South Africa's independence from the United Kingdom.
1948	Apartheid begins in South Africa.
1961	The Republic of South Africa is established, quitting the British Commonwealth.
1961	UN General Assembly refuses to recognize South Africa.
1962	UN General Assembly calls for sanctions against South Africa. Nelson Mandela announces a campaign of sabotage against government buildings.
1967	World's first heart transplant operation was conducted by South African surgeon Dr. Barnard.
1984	Desmond Tutu wins Nobel Peace Prize.
1989	Work begins to end apartheid. People of all races vote in parliamentary elections.
1990	Nelson Mandela is released from prison.
1992	Most European sanctions lifted. UN General Assembly ends certain restrictions.
1993	Most UN sanctions lifted. Constitution of the Republic of South Africa ratified.
1994	Apartheid is fully repealed. First democratic national election held. Nelson Mandela was elected president.
2015	South African government makes rules in an attempt to give farmland back to black farmers.
2019	Women were appointed to half the government's cabinet posts in South Africa.
Today	South Africa is still trying hard to work together, and create new ideas.

Printed in the United States
by Baker & Taylor Publisher Services